Full Throttle

Viper

Tracy Maurer

Rourke
Publishing LLC
Vero Beach, Florida 32964

www.rourkepublishing.com

AUTHOR CREDITS:
The author greatfully acknowledges project assistance provided by John Archer and his team (especially webmaster Jeremy at Archer Racing Accessories in Duluth, Minnesota.)

Also, the author extends appreciation to Jay Herbert, Mike Maurer, Lois M. Nelson, Margaret and Thomas, and the team at Rourke.

PHOTO CREDITS: © DigitalVision: page 11 (inset); Courtesy of DaimlerChrysler: all others

Editor: Robert Stengard-Olliges
Cover Design: Todd Field
Page Design: Nicola Stratford

Library of Congress Cataloging-in-Publication Data

Maurer, Tracy, 1965-
 Viper : full throttle / Tracy Maurer.
   p. cm. -- (Full throttle)
 Includes index.
 ISBN 1-60044-228-5 (hardcover)
 ISBN 978-1-60044-368-8 (paperback)
 1. Viper automobile--History--Juvenile literature.   I. Title.
TL215.V544M38 2007
629.222'2--dc22

2006020314

Printed in the USA

CG/CG

Rourke Publishing

www.rourkepublishing.com – sales@rourkepublishing.com
Post Office Box 3328, Vero Beach, FL 32964

Table of Contents

The New Muscle Car Era

The powerful Shelby Cobra revved up the first muscle car era in 1962. Thirty years later, Carroll Shelby, the Shelby Cobra's builder, helped unveil a new American muscle car: the Dodge Viper RT/10 Roadster. The first-generation Viper's wicked V-10 engine topped out at 166 miles (267 km) per hour. Raw power ruled again.

1992 First Generation: Viper RT/10 Roadster

The first Vipers had no roof and no glass side windows—just loads of power.

1996 Second Generation: Viper GTS Coupe & Viper GTS-R

The new Viper GTS Coupe sported new color options and a fastback body with better **aerodynamics**. Dodge also replaced the Roadster's cloth top with a removable hardtop. The GTS-R, strictly a racecar, snatched trophies everywhere.

The two-seater Viper RT/10 Roadster clocked 60 miles (96.5 km) per hour in just 4.6 seconds. It was the first American-made road car to accelerate faster than Shelby's 1966 AC Cobra.

aerodynamics
engineering designs that allow air to flow easily over the body for greater speed

torque
the force that causes an object to turn; usually measured in pound-feet (lb-ft)

A "V-10" engine has 10 fuel-burning cylinders in a V shape.

2003 Third Generation: Viper GTS-R Competition Coupe, Viper SRT-10 Roadster & Viper SRT-10 Coupe

This generation snarls with the "Three 500s" under the hood— 500 horsepower and **torque** measured at 525 pound-feet from the 505-cubic-inch V-10 engine. The cars look more stylish, too.

Dodge named its new speed demon "Viper" and used a snake logo to honor its ties to the 1960s Cobra.

Building a Winner

New cars take years to develop. Engineers and machinists use special drawings and research data to build a working model called a **prototype**. Then the carmaker tests and tweaks the design. Most factory-built cars look very little like their prototypes. The Viper team built a winner that looked very much like the hot prototype.

In 1990, the second Viper prototype, VM02, hinted at the real thing. Painted red, it had a rear sports bar and sleek, low windshield. A monster-sized V-10 engine rated at 380 **horsepower** rumbled under the hood.

People sent orders to buy the first Vipers before they were even built.

The first Viper prototype was built in a shop called the Snake Pit.

prototype
> for carmakers, the first working model of a design

horsepower
> a measure of mechanical power; one horsepower equals 550 pounds (885 kg) lifted at one foot (30.5 cm) per second

The Viper GTS Coupe prototype created a buzz at the 1993 North American Auto Show in Detroit.

Today's Brute

Today's Viper cranks out 500 horsepower with its brutal 8.3-liter V-10 engine. Both the SRT-10 Roadster and Coupe deliver more room, more strength, and better brakes than older models, too.

Early Viper engineers felt that anti-lock braking systems, or ABS, were too techy for their new muscle car—although most cars have ABS for safety.

Engineers finally added ABS to the Viper in 2001. Now a Viper SRT-10 brakes from 60 miles (97 km) per hour down to 0 in less than 100 feet (31 m). What goes fast must stop fast!

A Viper SRT-10 can charge from 0 to 100 miles (161 km) per hour and pull back to 0 in under 12.5 seconds.

2006 SRT "Trunk"

The 2006 hatchback trunk is nearly double the size of the 1996 Coupe's trunk (which means it now has enough room for a trophy—maybe).

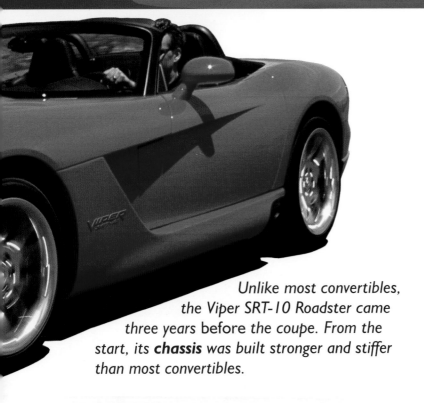

chassis
> the frame that supports the body of a vehicle

Unlike most convertibles, the Viper SRT-10 Roadster came three years before the coupe. From the start, its **chassis** *was built stronger and stiffer than most convertibles.*

Engineers used a plastic model wearing a race helmet to make sure the double-bubbled roof added enough headroom. The height also leaves room for a racing safety cage later.

Rear-Wheel Power

Most regular cars today use front-wheel drive. Their front wheels pull the car forward and steer.

Like most sports cars, the Viper uses rear-wheel drive. The engine power transfers to the rear wheels to push the car forward. Rear wheels don't steer, so they mainly deliver speed. Rear-wheel drive also helps balance the car's weight and hold the car steady during the Viper's fast acceleration.

The Viper gains stability and control from the back wing, or spoiler. It directs air downward to keep the car from lifting off the road at speeds above 100 miles (161 km) per hour.

The term "spoiler" comes from airplanes, which use wing flaps called spoilers to reduce speed and to land. Most spoilers on street cars do nothing except look cool.

The SRT-10 Coupe's wide spoiler helps catch 100 pounds (202 kg) of downforce at 150 miles (242 km) per hour.

Since the 1980s, carmakers have ditched rear-wheel drive on most regular cars because it costs more to build. Many drivers now prefer front-wheel drive, too. They think it gives them better control on slippery roads.

Find the Viper Code

To learn exactly when a certain Viper was built, look for a sticker below the latch on the driver's door. The Month-Day-Hour (MDH) sticker uses a special code that assigns two digits each for the month, day, and 24-hour time.

For example, a MDH sticker that says 031213 means:

03 = March, the third month

12 = the twelfth day

13 = 1:00 p.m., the thirteenth hour on a 24-hour clock.

Unlike most vehicles, the Viper does not use serial vehicle identification numbers (VINs) to show the order of when the car was built.

NBC tapped into the Viper's appeal when it cast the car as a crime-fighting machine in a TV show. The "Defender" car had more fans than the short-lived show did. A different Viper later made its way to the big screen in the 2003 movie sequel, 2Fast 2Furious.

Fast Fact

Less than 2,000 Vipers have been built each year at the Conner Avenue Assembly Plant in Detroit, Michigan.

American workers, often in teams of five, have built one Dodge Viper at a time in the European sports car tradition.

The Heart of the Beast

The rumor stops here: The Viper does not have a truck engine. (However, Viper's third-generation V-10 engine is at the heart of Dodge Ram SRT-10 pickups. But that's a different story.)

The rumor started back in 1987. Dodge's truck engineers added two cylinders to the V-8 engine in the Ram pickup. Then Team Viper stuffed a version of that Ram V-10 cast-iron engine under the hood of the prototype shown at the 1989 Detroit International Auto Show. But it was just for the show. The heart of the Viper is truly its own beast.

Viper Engines

Viper engineers used aluminum to reduce the engine's weight. They added strength and boosted horsepower.

More weight on a car usually means less speed.

World-Class Speedster

The 2003 Viper Competition Coupe weighed 2,995 pounds (1,360 kg) and clocked 0 to 60 miles (97 km) per hour in 3.7 seconds. Three years later, the SRT Coupe weighed a hefty 3,410 pounds (1,546 kg). It still nailed 0 to 60 miles (97 km) per hour in less than four seconds.

Motor Highlights

The third-generation Viper V-10 engine spews raw power like a snake spits venom.
* Huge 8.3-liter engine
* Top speed of 190 miles (312 km) per hour
* Biggest gasoline motor made in the U.S.
* Burns only high-octane fuel
* Needs about 11 quarts of oil (a normal car uses between three and five quarts)
* Draws nearly four gallons of coolant (a normal car holds about two gallons)

From the start, a manual six-speed transmission has been the only option for a Viper. No sissy automatic transmissions here! Shifting the gears gives the driver more control.

Fast Fact

The SRT Coupe ranks as one of the world's fastest-accelerating cars.

Two Hot Cats

American-made cars must use **catalytic converters**, or cats, in the exhaust systems to reduce harmful pollution. Cats use metal-coated chambers to change the pollution's chemistry before the exhaust leaves the car. The process is hot. Each of the two cats in the Viper exhaust system burns at about 1,600° F (871° C).

catalytic converter
a device that helps change toxic pollution from an engine's exhaust into harmless gas and liquid

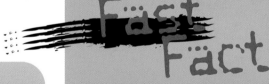

Catalytic converters first appeared in the mid-1970s. Now most cars use at least two cats in their exhaust systems.

Sidepipes

The Viper's well-tuned dual exhaust sidepipes rumble like a hungry tractor on steroids. To meet noise laws, engineers crisscrossed the pipes like an "X" under the passenger seats. Heat—LOTS of heat—rises from the pipes and the catalytic converters. The cockpit feels mighty toasty after a few fast miles.

Brawny Style

The Viper looks more brawny than beautiful. Its long nose and short rear follow the basic sports car shape. It's not as curvy as the fancy European models, but the fenders do bulge like well-pumped biceps. Both the Roadster and Coupe versions cut a low and slinky profile. The front windshield's swept-back angle adds to the Viper's full-throttle attitude, too.

Color Milestones

Serious drivers care a lot more about exciting performance than exciting color choices. Although Dodge has dabbled in a few options, red is still the main Viper color.

Model Year	Color Milestone
1992	Any color as long as it's red
1993	Red or black
1994	Red, black, yellow, or green
1996	Blue with white stripe
1998	White with blue stripe (special edition)
2002	Red with white stripe (special edition)
2006	Red, of course; black, yellow, or blue

2006 SRT-10 COUPE HOOD VENTS

Not just for style, the air vents on the 2006 SRT-10 suck air directly to the filters inside. The five angled vents on each side of the hood represent the five cylinders on each side of the V-10 engine.

The Rolling Stock

From 1992 to 1996, the Viper sported a unique three-spoke, 17-inch (43 cm) wheel design and special tires. By 2006, the rear wheels had grown to a mammoth 19 inches (48.25 cm). Buyers could choose either five-spoke or H-spoke wheels. The latest Michelin-made tires use run-flat technology, so the tires won't fwop-fwop-fwop without air and drivers don't need to carry a heavy spare tire.

Like most performance racecars, the Dodge Viper SRT-10 uses a red pushbutton starter to fire up the V-10. Other racing touches include the center-mounted tachometer and 220-mph speedometer.

The sharp crosshair or "plus sign" design on the Viper grille started a trend. Now all Dodge products have the Viper grille, even minivans.

Buyers have snapped up every special-edition Viper. The 1998 GT2 Championship Edition, honoring the 1997 FIA GT2 race victory, wore white paint with blue stripes and a tall rear wing. All 100 sold out immediately.

Painted red with white stripes, the Viper 2002 GTS Final Edition was also a fast sell-out. Dodge built only 360 special GTS cars to mark the end of that coupe's design.

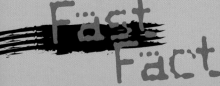

Fast Fact

In 2002, Dodge gave current Viper owners first dibs at ordering the new 2003 Viper SRT-10 Convertible. The first year's production—about 1,800 cars—sold out immediately.

Race Ready

Dodge put its V-10 to the racing test with the Viper GTS-R. It blew away the competition, especially at 24-hour **endurance** races. The Viper GTS-R captured five international GT championships between 1997 and 2000. Winning the 2000 Rolex 24 at Daytona left a mark in the history books. Viper won its class and the entire race—the first for an American factory racecar.

The Michelin Challenge Series, part of Viper Days, is a national competition for club racers. For advanced drivers, the Viper Racing League hosts wheel-to-wheel races.

RACING MILESTONES

1997, 1998, 1999	FIA GT2 class championships
1998	24 Hours of Le Mans Series GT2 class title
1999, 2000	American Le Mans Series GTS class titles
2000	Daytona Rolex 24
2004	SCCA Formula D (Drifting) Championship

drifting
skidding or sliding at high speeds in a performance car

endurance
power or strength to keep going or continue for a long time or distance

Viper was the first American-made vehicle to win a **drifting** competition.

The Viper GTS-R won many races. Its non-racing version, the GTS Coupe, was the official pace car for the 1996 Indianapolis 500.

DODGE

28
00

OFFICIAL PACE CAR
80TH INDIANAPOLIS 500 MAY 26 1996

America's Production Race Car

In 2002, DaimlerChrysler tapped its own speed freaks and mechanical wizards to form a new Performance Vehicle Operations (PVO) team. These creative engineers soon presented their first of many heart-stoppers: the Viper Competition Coupe. It was the first American race-ready car delivered straight from the factory.

The Viper Competition Coupe accelerated from 0 to 60 miles (97 km) per hour in 3.7 seconds and screamed from 0 to 100 miles (161 km) per hour in 9.2 seconds. Its top speed hit 193 miles (311 km) per hour.

Race-Ready Fresh from the Factory

- Just one racing seat with six-point safety belts
- Race instruments on lightweight dashboard
- Side-window netting
- Fire extinguishers
- Safety cage or roll cage
- Braces over the engine
- 25-gallon padded fuel cell
- 18-inch Hoosier racing slicks

Viper Competition Coupes are not **street-legal**. *Drivers can run them only on a racetrack. Club racing allows drivers to race against the clock.*

primer
    a base paint that seals
    the surface
street-legal
    a vehicle allowed to be
    driven on a city streets
    because it meets the
    standards set by law

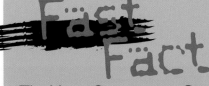

The Viper Competition Coupe arrives with **primer** and no paint. The owner hires a special painter to finish the car in the racing team's colors.

No Joe Schmoes

The Viper plant in Livonia, Michigan, has made less than 60 Viper Competition Coupes in a year. The price tags started at $130,000. Only approved race drivers or race teams could buy them—not Regular Joe Schmoes.

Viper owners who want to race can take lessons at high-performance driving schools. The Viper Club of America hosts a Viper driving school during Viper Days, a national event for Viper owners and fans.

Not everyone can afford a Viper. But Viper fans everywhere easily bring home the many different Viper toys and model cars. Special collector shows let hardcore Viper fans buy, sell, and trade their Viper stuff, too.

aftermarket
  parts added to a
  vehicle after its sale to
  the owner

A custom shop rips out
about 40 pounds (18 kg)
of sound-proofing
material to make a street
car lighter for racing.

Special shops add **aftermarket** parts to customize Vipers. With the right aftermarket gear, owners can boost the V-10 up to 880 horsepower. Some shops also strip street cars and turn them into racecars.

Many of America's classic muscle car legends returned to the motoring scene after Viper paved the way. With its power and speed, Viper is well down the road to its place in motoring history.

Glossary

aerodynamics (ahr oh dih NAM iks) – engineering designs that allow air to flow easily over the body for greater speed

aftermarket (AFF tur MAR kit) – parts added to a vehicle after its sale to the owner

catalytic converter (kat ah LIT ik cahn VUR tur) – a device that helps change toxic pollution from an engine's exhaust into harmless gas and liquid

chassis (CHASS ee) – the frame that supports the body of a vehicle

drifting (DRIF ting) – skidding or sliding at high speeds in a performance car

endurance (en DUR ahns) – power or strength to keep going or continue for a long time or distance

horsepower (HORS pow ur) – a measure of mechanical power; one horsepower equals 550 pounds (885 kg) lifted at one foot (30.5 cm) per second

torque (TORK) – the force that causes an object to turn; usually measured in pound-feet (lb-ft)

primer (PRIH mur) – a base paint that seals the surface

prototype (PROH tah tihp) – for carmakers, the first working model of a design

street-legal (STREET LEE gahl) – a vehicle allowed to be driven on city streets because it meets the standards set by law

Further Reading

Henshaw, Peter. *Muscle Cars*. Thunder Bay Press, 2004.

Tracy Nelson Maurer. *Roaring Rides: Muscle Cars.*
   Rourke Publishing, 2004.

Adam Phillips. *Supercars: Driving the Dream.*
   Barnes and Noble Books, 2006.

Matt F.G.A. Stone. *Viper.* MBI Publishing, 2004.

Websites

www.dodge.com/viper

www.viperclub.org

www.viperdays.com

www.vipermagazine.com

Index

About the Author

Tracy Nelson Maurer writes nonfiction and fiction books for children, including more than 50 titles for Rourke Publishing LLC. Tracy lives with her husband Mike and two children near Minneapolis, Minnesota.

I didn't know that some plants grow in mid-air

© Aladdin Books Ltd 1998
Produced by
Aladdin Books Ltd
28 Percy Street
London W1P 0LD

ISBN 0-7496-3114-7
First published in Great Britain in 1998 by
Aladdin Books/Watts Books
96 Leonard Street
London EC2A 4RH

Concept, editorial and design by

David West 🧍🧍 Children's Books

Designer: Robert Perry
Illustrators: Myke Taylor – Wildlife Art Ltd.,
Jo Moore

Printed in Belgium

I didn't know that some plants grow in mid-air

Claire Llewellyn

A l a d d i n / W a t t s
London • Sydney

I didn't know that

Introduction

Did *you* know that the rafflesia is the biggest flower in the world? ... that chimpanzees get food with stones and twigs? ... that the arrow-poison frogs' bright colours mean 'keep away'?

Discover for yourself amazing facts about rainforests, from their spotted cats to their towering trees – and find out what we can do to ensure their future.

 Look out for this symbol which means there is a fun project for you to try.

Is it true or is it false? Watch for this symbol and try to answer the question before reading on for the answer.

I didn't know that

it can rain every day in a rainforest. Tropical rainforests grow in places where the weather is so hot and sticky and there's a rainstorm nearly every day. The warm, wet weather is perfect for plants – they just grow, and grow and grow!

Can you find two monkeys?

SEARCH & FIND • FIND & SEARCH

Rainforest areas

Tropical rainforests are found near the *equator* in the warmest parts of the world. The largest is the Amazonian rainforest in South America; it's almost 30 times bigger than the U.K.

In an equatorial rainforest it rains at the same time every day.

True or false?
Rainforest plants rot in the rain.

Answer: **False**

Rainforest plants don't go soggy in the rain.
The leaves are tough and shiny, and have
drip tips that make drainpipes
for the rain.

Put a plastic bag
over a houseplant
and leave it in a warm
place. The plant gives off
water, the bag begins to
mist and water 'rains'
down the sides. This
happens in a rainforest.

Squirrel monkey

7

Tallest trees in emergent layer

The trees' branches spread out to form a *canopy* over the forest. Birds, monkeys and other animals live up here, flying, leaping or swinging from branch to branch.

Canopy

SEARCH & FIND
FIND & SEARCH
Can you find five jaguars?

It is damp and shady below the canopy. Small trees and huge ferns grow here. Large flowers show up in the gloom.

Understorey

Shrub layer

I didn't know that

the world's tallest trees grow in rainforests. Some rainforest trees are up to 80 m high – about twice as high as most church spires. They grow this tall to reach the sunlight, which gives them the *energy* they need to survive.

True or false?

Rainforest trees have very long roots.

Answer: **False**

Rainforest trees have short roots because the soil is poor and contains little goodness. To hold up the trees, strong supports called buttress roots grow around the base of the trunk.

9

Sword-billed hummingbird

I didn't know that

hummingbirds drink from flowers. Hummingbirds are tiny birds that feed on rainforest flowers. They hover in mid-air, beating their wings very fast. They put their long beaks inside the petals and suck up the *nectar*.

Butterflies have long tongues to reach the nectar in flowers.

The toucan uses its long beak to reach fruit at the end of a branch.

The quetzal feeds on the fruit of the avocado tree. It spits out the fruit's hard stone. The stone will grow into a new avocado tree.

SEARCH & FIND & FIND & SEARCH

Can you find the stick insect?

To grow an avocado stone pierce it with toothpicks, and hang it on a jam-jar with the base of the stone in water. When roots grow, plant it in *compost* and put it in a sunny place.

Avocado stone

Jam-jar

Tooth-picks

Water

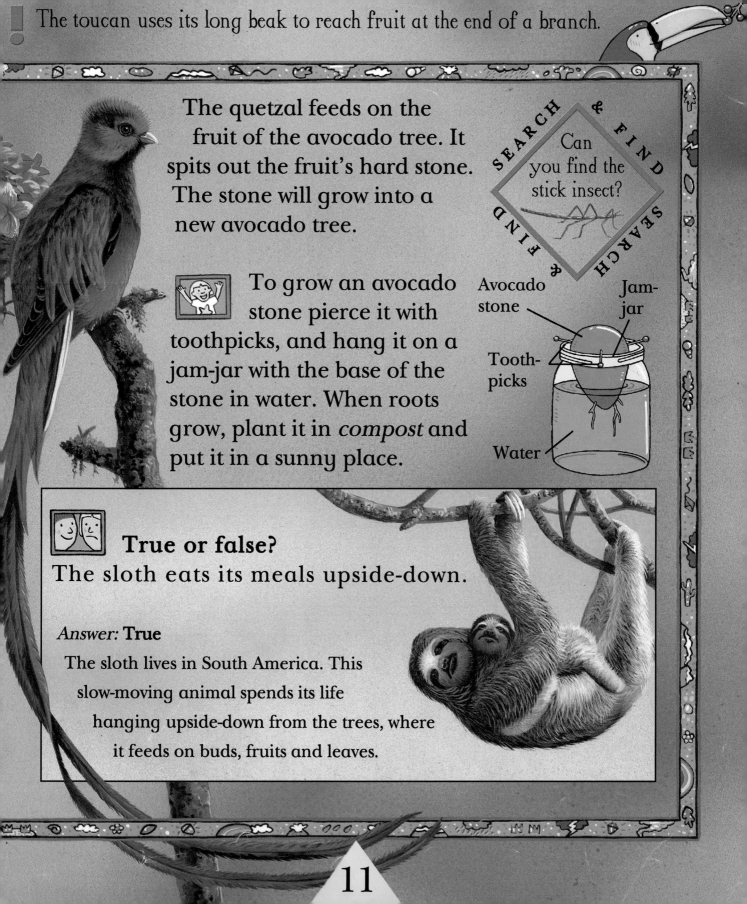

True or false?
The sloth eats its meals upside-down.

Answer: **True**
The sloth lives in South America. This slow-moving animal spends its life hanging upside-down from the trees, where it feeds on buds, fruits and leaves.

Large wandering spiders creep through the trees, hunting for frogs, lizards and snakes. They even catch birds as they sit on their nests.

Leopard

True or false?
Rainforest eagles are the biggest in the world.

Answer: **True**
The huge harpy eagles of South America stand about one metre tall. They sail over the canopy, using their massive claws and strong, hooked beaks to catch birds, monkeys and sloths.

12

The emerald tree boa eats tree frogs and their eggs. It has no trouble climbing a tree. When it wants to rest, the snake coils itself around the branch.

SEARCH & FIND
Can you find the leaf insect?
FIND & SEARCH

I didn't know that

leopards ambush their prey. Leopards live in the forests of Africa and Asia, and hide silently in the trees. As soon as an animal passes below, these big cats drop down and kill their prey.

Water chevrotain

! Hordes of army ants attack small animals on the forest floor.

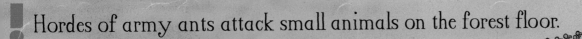

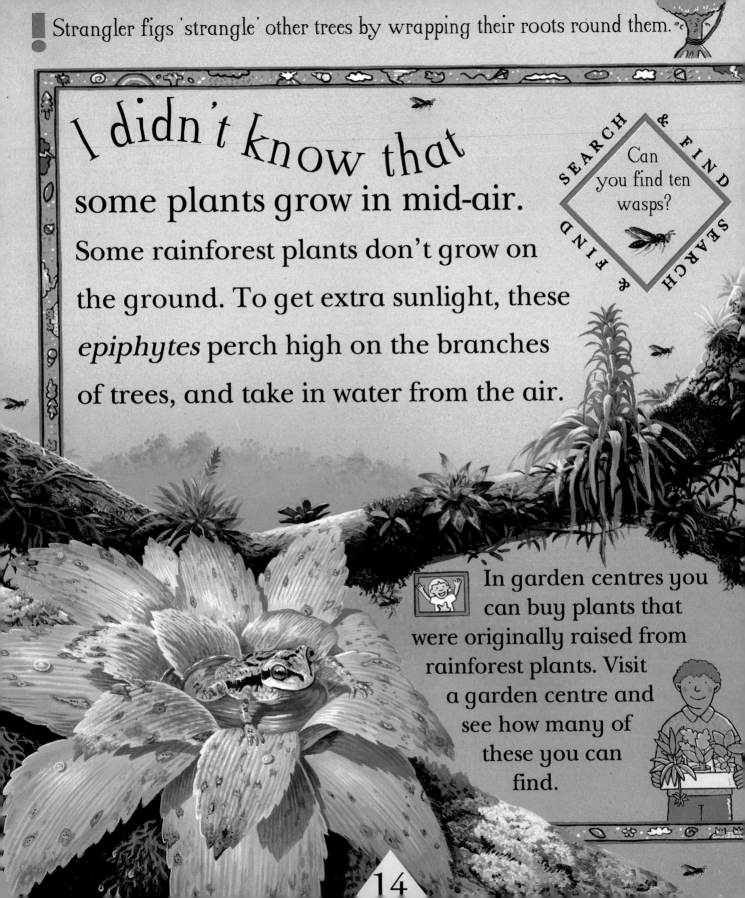

I didn't know that

some plants grow in mid-air.

Some rainforest plants don't grow on the ground. To get extra sunlight, these *epiphytes* perch high on the branches of trees, and take in water from the air.

SEARCH & FIND
Can you find ten wasps?
FIND & SEARCH

In garden centres you can buy plants that were originally raised from rainforest plants. Visit a garden centre and see how many of these you can find.

The spectacular rafflesia is the smelliest flower in the world. Its foul odour helps to attract flies, which then spread the flower's pollen.

True or false?
Some plants eat meat.

Answer: **True**

Pitcher plants have slippery, vase-shaped leaves that give off a sugar-sweet smell. When an insect lands on the plant, it slips down into the vase. There, it drowns and dissolves in a juice, which the plant slowly drinks.

An Amazon water lily's leaf is strong enough to hold a child.

Tarzan of the Apes tells the story of a boy who is brought up by apes in the rainforest, and even learns to swing through the trees.

Orang-utan

I didn't know that

old men climb through the trees. 'Orang-utan' is a *Malay* word that means 'old man of the forest'. Orang-utan are rare apes that live in south-east Asia. Their strong arms and hooked fingers help them move through the trees.

! On the ground, gibbons lift their long arms to help them to balance.

Chimpanzees are small apes in the forests of Africa. They are clever animals, and have learned to use simple tools, such as stones to smash nuts, and twigs to catch termites inside their nests.

 True or false? Gorillas are fierce animals.

The South American spider monkey has a strong, muscular tail which it uses to hang from the trees. It can even pick nuts with it!

Answer: **False**

Gorillas are not fierce. This is a myth that some films have helped to spread. They are peaceful animals unless disturbed or threatened. They live in family groups in the African rainforest, feeding on fresh fruit and leaves.

I didn't know that

some trees grow on stilts.

Mangrove trees grow in places where rainforests meet the sea. They have strong roots like stilts, which support them as they stand above the muddy *swamps* and the swirling, salty tides.

SEARCH & FIND
Can you find the mangrove snake?
FIND & SEARCH

Saltwater crocodiles live around the coasts of south-east Asia. They are the world's largest crocodiles, and can measure eight metres from snout to tail. They are strong enough to attack and kill young tigers!

Mudskipper

True or false?
Some fish can climb trees.

Answer: **True**
At low tide, mudskipper fish leave the swamp, prop themselves up on their strong, fleshy fins, and crawl over the mud. The fish carry water in their gills to breathe, and even climb trees in their search for food.

This muddy swamp is full of leaves and tiny plants and animals. At low tide, a huge army of fiddler crabs comes out to feed on the feast.

Meat-eating piranhas live in the rainforest rivers.

I didn't know that

some frogs are poisonous.
The arrow-poison frog's skin contains
a strong poison that deters its enemies
from eating it. The frog warns its enemies of this
deadly weapon by being brightly
coloured, meaning 'keep away'.

SEARCH & FIND & FIND & SEARCH

Can you find eight frogs?

20

Birds with bright colours are easier to spot in the dark, shady forest. Male manakins have wonderful blue, green and yellow feathers, which help them attract a mate.

The eyed silkmoth has large, scary eyespots on its wings. When it is threatened by a hungry bird, the moth flashes its eyespots to confuse the enemy, and gives itself time to escape.

A gaboon viper's speckly skin hides it on the forest floor.

Flying fox

I didn't know that

foxes fly in the jungle. The large
fruit bats of south-east Asia are also
known as flying foxes. At night,
they fly long distances to feed on
ripe forest fruits.

SEARCH & FIND
Can you find ten fireflies?
FIND & SEARCH

Forests are noisy places at night - full of croaks, buzzes and squeaks.

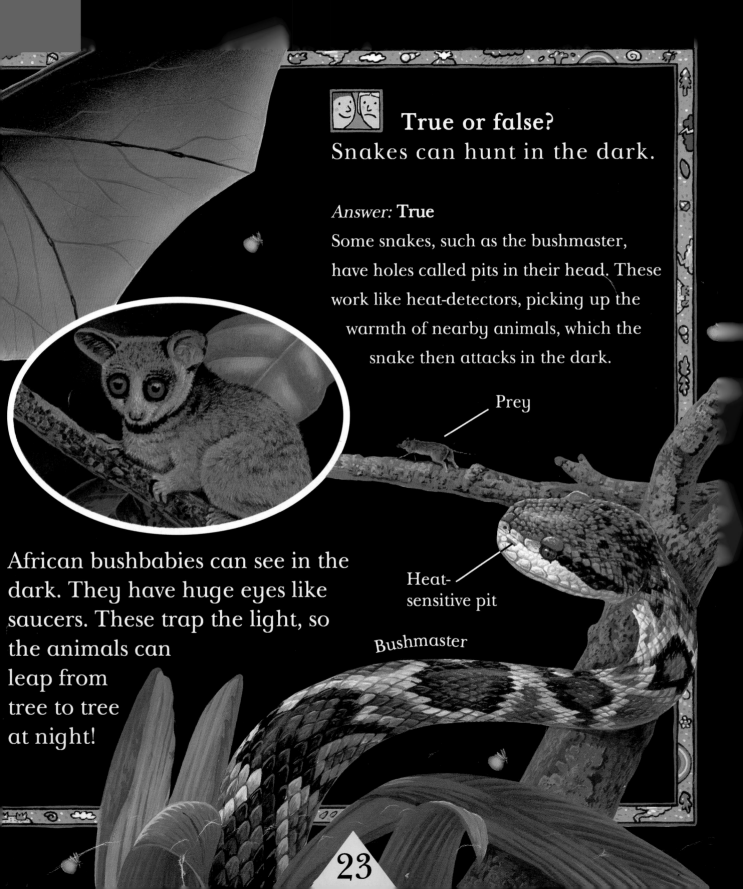

True or false?
Snakes can hunt in the dark.

Answer: **True**

Some snakes, such as the bushmaster, have holes called pits in their head. These work like heat-detectors, picking up the warmth of nearby animals, which the snake then attacks in the dark.

Prey

Heat-sensitive pit

Bushmaster

African bushbabies can see in the dark. They have huge eyes like saucers. These trap the light, so the animals can leap from tree to tree at night!

23

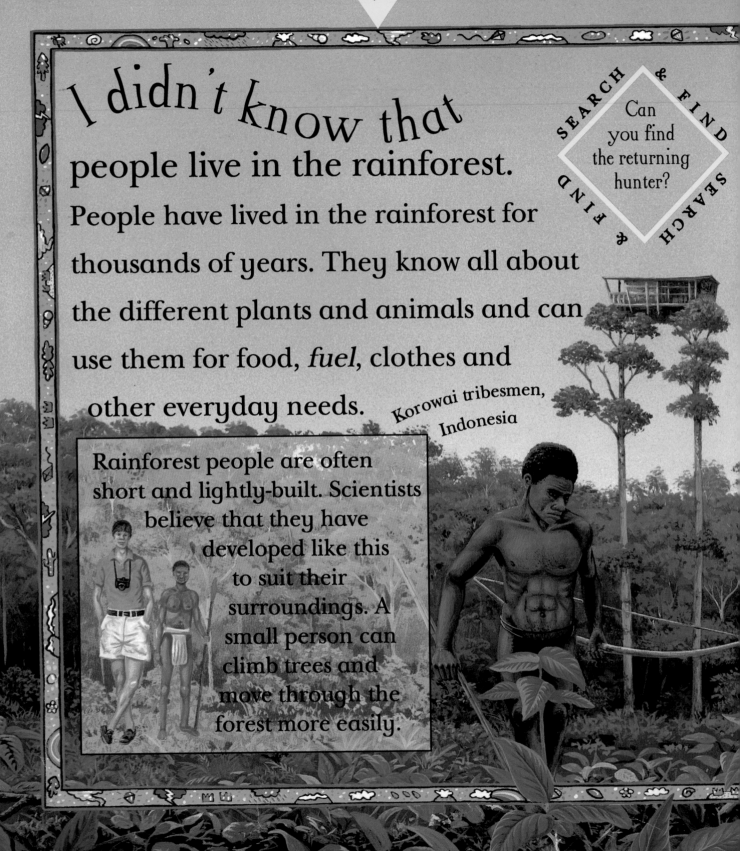

I didn't know that

people live in the rainforest.
People have lived in the rainforest for
thousands of years. They know all about
the different plants and animals and can
use them for food, *fuel*, clothes and
other everyday needs.

Korowai tribesmen,
Indonesia

Can
you find
the returning
hunter?

SEARCH & FIND & SEARCH & FIND

Rainforest people are often
short and lightly-built. Scientists
believe that they have
developed like this
to suit their
surroundings. A
small person can
climb trees and
move through the
forest more easily.

There are so many rivers in a rainforest that the easiest way to get around is by boat. Canoes are made by hollowing out tree trunks and logs.

Hunting in the forest takes practice, time and skill. Hunters kill animals using either long *blowpipes* or bows and arrows. They dip the tips of their darts and arrows into deadly poisons, which they make from animals and plants.

I didn't know that

rainforests are in danger. People are cutting down huge parts of the rainforest. They sell the trees and then burn the land to clear it for cattle, crops and *mines*.

As the trees are cut down, animals lose their homes and their numbers begin to shrink. There are only about 150 golden lion tamarins left in the wild, and the animal may soon be *extinct*.

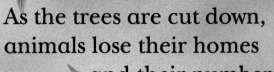

Can you find the parrot?

SEARCH & FIND

FIND & SEARCH

True or false?
Tourists can help the rainforest.

Answer: **True**

Small groups of tourists can help the rainforests. '*Eco-tourists*' respect the forests and want to learn about the animals and plants. The money they pay is used to protect endangered animals.

Planes drop 'bombs' of seeds on the rainforests to resow them.

I didn't know that

rainforest plants save lives.

Rainforest plants fight off harmful *pests* by producing special chemicals. Scientists now use these chemicals in medicines to fight disease. A quarter of our medicines come from rainforest plants.

A lot of the food we eat originally came from a rainforest. Go to the supermarket and look for some rainforest food.

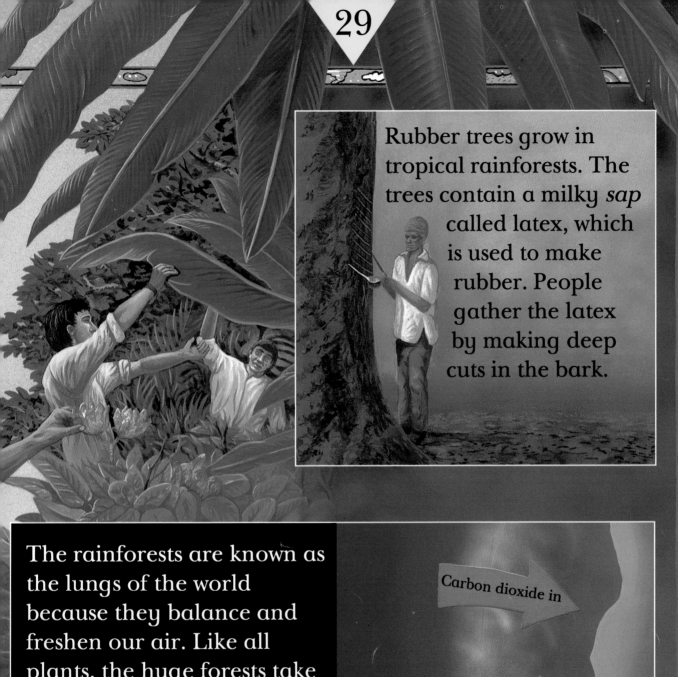

Rubber trees grow in tropical rainforests. The trees contain a milky *sap* called latex, which is used to make rubber. People gather the latex by making deep cuts in the bark.

The rainforests are known as the lungs of the world because they balance and freshen our air. Like all plants, the huge forests take in carbon dioxide from the air and give out oxygen – the gas we all need to survive.

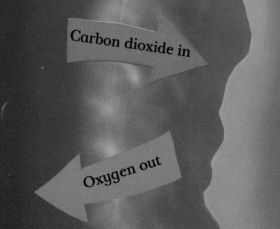

Carbon dioxide in

Oxygen out

Scientists use rock-climbing equipment to explore the towering forests.

Glossary

Blowpipe
A hollow tube used by hunters to blow poisoned darts.

Canopy
The top layer of a rainforest, made up of the leaves and branches of the tallest trees.

Compost
A nourishing soil made from rotted-down plants.

Drip tip
The long point at the end of a leaf.

Eco-tourist
A tourist who wishes to support and observe the natural world.

Energy
The strength to live and grow. Rainforest trees make the Sun's energy into sugars for growth.

Epiphyte
A plant that grows on another plant. An epiphyte uses the other plant as a support, but does not harm it.

quator
n imaginary line around the
ddle of the Earth, halfway
tween the North and South
les.

xtinct
n animal is extinct when it no
nger lives on the Earth.

uel
material, such as wood or
al, that we burn to produce
eat or power.

alay
he language of Malaysia in
uth-east Asia.

ine
here coal or
her materials
e dug from
e Earth.

Nectar
The sweet liquid inside flowers,
which attracts insects, birds
and bats.

Pest
A small animal that harms or
destroys plants.

Sap
The juice that carries food
around inside a plant.

Swamp
Soft, wet, muddy
land.

Index